ANIMATION

FROM CONCEPT TO CONSUMER

BY JOSH GREGORY

CHILDREN'S PRESS®

An Imprint of Scholastic Inc.
New York Toronto London Auckland Sydney
Mexico City New Delhi Hong Kong
Danbury, Connecticut

CONTENT CONSULTANT
Robert St. Pierre, Production Designer, Background Layout Artist, Walt Disney Animation Studios
and Assistant Professor of Animation, California State University, Northridge

PHOTOGRAPHS ©: Alamy Images: 14 right, 33 (AF archive), 24 (Clynt Garnham Products), 51
(EuroStyle Graphics), 10 left (INSADCO Photography), 15, 20, 22, 31 (Moviestore collection Ltd),
40 (Phil Rees), 16 (Photos 12), 27 (Pictorial Press Ltd), 56 (RGB Ventures LLC dba SuperStock),
36, 50 (ZUMA Press, Inc.); AP Images: 6 (Dreamworks Animation), 46 (Jordan Strauss/Invision),
18 (Pizac, Pizac); Corbis Images/Bettmann: 11 right; Everett Collection: 55 (20th Century Fox
Film Corp.), 10 right, 11 left (AISA), 32 (Cartoon Network), 29 (Columbia Pictures),
26, 34 (Dreamworks), 8 (Mary Evans Picture Library), 39, 52 (Paramount Pictures), 5 right,
53 (Paramount), 19 (Pixar Animation Studios), 30 (Sony Pictures), 3, 58 bottom, 59 left
(Warner Bros. Pictures), 28 (Warner Bros.), 17; Getty Images/Tony Bock: 5 left, 43 right;
Kingcoma represented by Artbox: cover; Media Bakery: 54, 57, 59 right; Photofest: 37, 45
(Disney-Pixar), 58 top (Walt Disney Pictures), 12; Shutterstock, Inc.: 25 (asife), 48 (auremar);
Superstock, Inc.: 4 right, 23 (Walt Disney Animation Studios), 13 (Walt Disney Pictures);
The Image Works: 41 (Andrew Cooper/Paramount/Columbia Pictures/Archives du 7e Art/
Photo12), 9 (Mary Evans Picture Library), 43 left (Pixar/TopFoto), 44 (RIA Novosti), 42
(Sam Urdank/Universal Pictures/Archives du 7e Art/Photo12), 4 left, 14 left, 49 (TopFoto).

LIBRARY OF CONGRESS CATALOGING-IN-PUBLICATION DATA
Gregory, Josh.
 Animation : from concept to consumer / by Josh Gregory.
  pages cm. — (Calling all innovators : a career for you)
 Includes bibliographical references and index.
 ISBN 978-0-531-20613-3 (lib. bdg.) — ISBN 978-0-531-21072-7 (pbk.)
 1. Animated films—Vocational guidance—Juvenile literature. 2. Animation
(Cinematography)—Vocational guidance—Juvenile literature. I. Title.
 NC1765.G74 2014
 741.5'8023—dc23   2014003566

1 2 3 4 5 6 7 8 9 10 R 24 23 22 21 20 19 18 17 16 15

Science, technology, engineering, arts, and math are the fields that drive innovation. Whether they are finding ways to make our lives easier or developing the latest entertainment, the people who work in these fields are changing the world for the better. Do you have what it takes to join the ranks of today's greatest innovators? Read on to discover whether animation is a career for you.

TABLE *of* CONTENTS

Ub Iwerks worked with Walt Disney for many years.

Animating Disney's Frozen *required the creation of new software.*

Foley artists add many of the background sounds to films.

An animator plans out a scene using simplified models called proxies.

The details in the animation found in films such as 2014's Mr. Peabody and Sherman can take a team of animators years to complete.

CHAPTER ONE

UP ON THE SCREEN

Dad flips off the light switch as he carries a heaping bowl of fresh popcorn into the living room. The rest of the family has already settled into favorite spots on the couch, and the TV is glowing. It's movie night! As Mom pushes the play button on the remote, everyone gets ready for the opening credits to roll. Soon, the movie's colorful cartoon characters are talking, singing, and running around in a detailed fantasy world as their hilarious, action-packed story unfolds. The characters were made using computer-generated animation, and they are remarkably expressive. Their cartoon faces show a wide range of emotions, and they move smoothly through a variety of settings. The family laughs, cries, and shouts in excitement as it watches what happens on the screen.

EARLY ACHIEVEMENTS

1832	1834	1906	1928
Joseph Plateau invents the phenakistoscope.	William George Horner introduces the zoetrope.	James Stuart Blackton releases Humorous Phases of Funny Faces.	Walt Disney releases Steamboat Willie.

FIRST STEPS

Today's animated movies take advantage of the latest technology to display realistic characters and detailed settings. However, the basic ideas behind this technology are far from cutting edge. Inventors dreamed up early forms of animation hundreds of years ago. In the 1600s, people built devices called magic lanterns. Magic lanterns were similar to more modern-day slide **projectors**. Operators placed hand-painted or photographic glass slides in their magic lanterns, and used candles or torches to shine light through them. This projected the images from the glass plates onto a wall or screen.

In 1832, Belgian inventor Joseph Plateau unveiled a device called a phenakistoscope (fen-uh-KIS-tuh-skope). A phenakistoscope was a circular piece of cardboard with a series of images printed around it. As users spun the device in front of a mirror, the reflected image seemed to move.

J. A. PARIS

In 1825, English physician John Ayrton Paris created the thaumatrope. This was a small disc with one image printed on the front and another on the back. A viewer rapidly spun the disc, causing its two images to apparently combine into one. The same optical illusion was later used in more complicated animation, from the phenakistoscope forward.

Phenakistoscopes created short, simple animations.

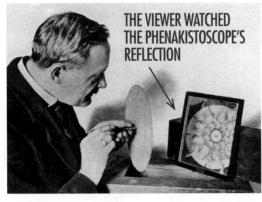

THE VIEWER WATCHED THE PHENAKISTOSCOPE'S REFLECTION

IN A LATER VERSION, THE VIEWER WATCHED THROUGH SLITS IN ANOTHER DISC.

HAND CRANK
TO TURN
THE THÉÂTRE
OPTIQUE

Émile Reynaud's invention was able to show animations that were several minutes long.

PUBLIC PERFORMANCE

William George Horner introduced an invention called a zoetrope
(ZOH-ee-trope) in 1834. A zoetrope was a cylinder with slits cut
into its sides. Strips of paper showing a series of images could be
wrapped around the inside. These images would appear to move
when a user spun the zoetrope and looked through its slits. Users
could change the animations by putting different strips of images
inside the zoetrope.

In the late 1800s, a French inventor named Émile Reynaud
expanded upon the principles of the magic lantern and animation toys
such as the phenakistoscope and the zoetrope to bring true animation
closer to reality. Reynaud's invention, called the Théâtre Optique,
used mirrors to project images from spinning cylinders onto a screen.
Thousands of people attended his shows during the late 1800s.

FIRST THINGS FIRST

Each individual image of a motion picture is called a **frame**. A motion picture must display several frames—typically 24—each second to create the illusion of motion. The more frames that are displayed each second, the smoother the motion will seem.

FROM FILM TO SCREEN

The invention of **film** made of flexible celluloid, a kind of plastic, allowed movies to be projected on screens. The frames of a movie are printed one after another on a **reel** of film. Equally spaced holes cut along both sides of the film align with the teeth of a **sprocket** on the projector. The sprocket spins, moving the film through the projector at a steady speed. A light shines through from behind the spinning film, projecting each frame onto a screen as the reel spins. Today, many filmmakers and movie theaters are switching to digital filming and projection. However, some still depend on traditional celluloid film.

The sprocket moves the film fast enough that the audience sees the illusion of motion.

MOVING PICTURES

Animation as we know it today developed alongside the earliest **live-action** movies in the late 1800s and early 1900s. Both animated and live-action motion pictures rely on a concept called persistence of vision. When the human eye sees a fast succession of images, the brain is fooled into seeing continuous motion between each image. This is because each image stays in the mind for a split second as the next one is displayed. The brain fills in any gaps between the images.

FILM PIONEERS

In the second half of the 19th century, a series of inventors developed the technology needed to film and project motion pictures. Brothers Auguste and Louis Lumière created one of the earliest functional movie cameras in 1895. The brothers used their invention to film workers as they left the Lumière factory. This film is considered to be the first true motion picture.

The Lumière brothers named their invention the cinematograph.

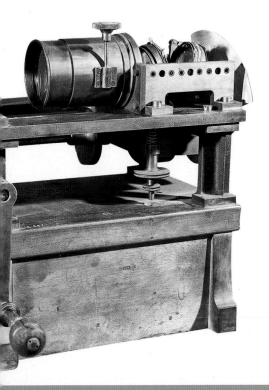

James Stuart Blackton cofounded the production company Vitagraph, which was incredibly successful in the early years of film.

THE FIRST ANIMATED FILMS

Each frame of a live-action movie is a single photographic image of actors performing on a set. Creative minds soon realized that movie frames could be made from drawings or paintings. One of the first creators to successfully produce animated films was James Stuart Blackton. Blackton was originally an illustrator and a journalist. He began making animated films in the 1890s after interviewing legendary inventor Thomas Edison, who had created one of the earliest motion picture cameras. ✳

Humorous Phases of Funny Faces was animated using simple, white line drawings on a black chalkboard.

NEW POSSIBILITIES

The earliest animated films were very simple. For example, Blackton's 1906 short film *Humorous Phases of Funny Faces* was made by filming a series of drawings on a chalkboard. It consists mainly of cartoon heads making various facial expressions.

As animated films rose in popularity during the early 1900s, creators experimented with different methods of animation. Blackton and others sometimes used a method known as stop-motion animation. Stop-motion animation is created by taking photos of clay models, dolls, or other physical objects. The objects are moved slightly in between each **exposure** of the film, creating the same effect as hand-drawn animation.

CREATING COLORFUL CHARACTERS

The most common form of animation soon came to be based on simple cartoon drawings. These cartoons were inspired by the artwork of newspaper comic strips. It was easy to draw the simple shapes of the characters over and over again to create many frames. Characters such as Felix the Cat and Gertie the Dinosaur became popular attractions on movie screens during the 1910s and 1920s.

In 1928, two animators named Walt Disney and Ub Iwerks released a short film that changed the world of animation forever. *Steamboat Willie* starred a new cartoon character named Mickey Mouse. In addition to introducing this legendary character, it was the first animated film to have a soundtrack that matched up with the action on-screen. The film was a huge hit, and Disney soon became the world's most successful animator.

Disney's Steamboat Willie *introduced what became one of the world's most recognizable characters.*

Ub Iwerks sketches a drawing of Mickey Mouse.

A ROUGH START

As a high school student in Chicago, Illinois, Walt Disney hoped to become a newspaper cartoonist. In 1919, he moved to Kansas City, Missouri, where he worked as an artist and met fellow cartoonist Ub Iwerks. Three years later, Disney and Iwerks opened an animation studio and began making short films. However, they went bankrupt in 1923. Disney moved to Hollywood and partnered with his brother, Roy, to try again as an animator. He also hired Iwerks as an artist. One of their earliest successes was a character named Oswald the Lucky Rabbit. Aside from his long ears, Oswald had a strong resemblance to Mickey Mouse, the character that would eventually make Disney a household name.

Snow White and the Seven Dwarfs proved that audiences were interested in longer animated films.

WALT'S WONDERS

Today, the Walt Disney Company controls a worldwide entertainment empire. It produces everything from animated movies and TV shows to video games, pop music, and live theatrical performances. It even operates several of the world's biggest theme parks. It might be hard to believe, but all of this started with some simple animated short films!

Actor Dick Van Dyke dances with animated penguins in Mary Poppins.

A FULL-LENGTH FEATURE

Though he found great success with Mickey Mouse and other characters in his early short films, Disney saw the potential for something greater in animation. He saw it as an art form that could compete with live-action films in telling longer, more serious stories. Along with a massive team of animators, Disney began working on a film called *Snow White and the Seven Dwarfs*. Released in 1937, it was the first feature-length animated film. Many of its characters were realistic-looking humans, rather than the goofy cartoon animals that were common at the time. The film was a huge hit with critics and audiences, and full-length animated features soon became a common sight on movie theater marquees.

HIT AFTER HIT

Snow White's success encouraged Disney to continue making ambitious animated features. He pushed his animators to create more realistic movement in characters and more striking details in the settings. Many of Disney's films, such as *Pinocchio* (1940), *Bambi* (1942), and *Cinderella* (1950), were based on popular children's books and fairy tales. The film versions soon became more famous than the stories that inspired them.

In addition to animated films, Disney soon began producing live-action films. In films such as *Song of the South* (1946) and *Mary Poppins* (1964), he combined live-action footage with animation, allowing live actors to interact with cartoon characters on-screen. ✸

GETTING LOONEY

In 1930, the film production company Warner Bros. opened its own animation studio. Its first animators included Friz Freleng, Rudolf Ising, and Hugh Harman, who had all previously worked under Walt Disney. Talented animators such as Chuck Jones, Tex Avery, and Bob Clampett soon joined them. Together, these creative minds developed a wide range of long-lasting characters at Warner Bros., including Bugs Bunny, Daffy Duck, Porky Pig,

and many others. In the following decades, these characters starred in hundreds of short, comedic films in the *Looney Tunes* and *Merrie Melodies* series. These shorts were originally shown in movie theaters, where their outrageous jokes and cartoonish violence made them enormously popular. Later, they found a new audience when they were aired on television.

Bugs Bunny remains one of the most popular animated Warner Bros. characters.

Max Fleischer works on an animated short.

THE FABULOUS FLEISCHERS

Two other important innovators during the early decades of animation were the Fleischer brothers, Max and Dave. They began creating animated films in 1915 when Max invented a device called a rotoscope. Using a rotoscope, animators can trace drawings over the top of live-action footage. This allows them to use live actors as a guide for character's movements. The Fleischers used this process for many of their early creations during the 1920s, and animators still occasionally use it today.

By the 1930s, the Fleischer brothers ranked among the world's most successful animators. While Disney and other major animation studios created films that appealed mainly to children, the Fleischers often focused on more adult themes. Betty Boop and Popeye the Sailor are two of the brothers' most enduring characters.

William Hanna (right) and Joseph Barbera (left) created a wide range of animated television series.

SMALL SCREEN SUCCESS

With the invention of television, animated cartoons became a staple of many networks' programming schedules. The team of William Hanna and Joseph Barbera produced many of the most popular animated television shows. The two met while working for the animation department of Metro-Goldwyn-Mayer (MGM), one of Hollywood's biggest movie production companies. Hanna and Barbera created the popular *Tom and Jerry* series for MGM before striking out to create a production company of their own in 1957. From then until the 1980s, Hanna-Barbera dominated the world of animated TV shows with such hit series as *The Flintstones*, *The Jetsons*, *Scooby-Doo*, *The Yogi Bear Show*, and *The Smurfs*.

GOING DIGITAL

In 1979, *Star Wars* director George Lucas hired computer scientist Ed Catmull to help develop a **computer graphics** division of his film production company, Lucasfilm. At first, Catmull and the rest of the team worked to build new computer technology for creating and displaying graphics. In 1983, former Disney animator John Lasseter began working with the division. Lasseter began using the division's cutting-edge technology to create short animated films.

Soon afterward, Lucas sold the computer graphics division of Lucasfilm to Apple cofounder Steve Jobs, who turned it into an independent company named Pixar. At first, Jobs hoped that Pixar could design powerful new graphics **hardware**, but he soon grew more impressed with the short films that Lasseter was creating. Pixar began to focus more on animation than hardware. In 1988, Lasseter's short *Tin Toy* won an Academy Award. Soon after, the company formed a partnership with Disney to create feature-length animated movies using computer graphics.

Ed Catmull (left), Steve Jobs (center), and John Lasseter (right) helped bring Pixar to the forefront of animation technology.

Toy Story *was an enormous hit with people of all ages around the world.*

CHAPTER TWO

2

CURRENT CARTOONS

Pixar's first feature, 1995's *Toy Story*, was a blockbuster hit that generated hundreds of millions of dollars at the box office. Audiences were wowed by the movie's fresh new visual style and engaging story. *Toy Story* was also beloved by critics. It was nominated for three Academy Awards. John Lasseter was presented with a Special Achievement Oscar for leading the creation of the first feature-length computer-animated film.

Thanks to *Toy Story*'s success, computer animation became the hottest thing in Hollywood almost overnight. Major movie studios launched their own computer animation departments to compete with Disney and Pixar. Since then, computer-animated films have grown to be a major part of the movie industry, drawing millions upon millions of viewers to movie theaters every year.

ANIMATED BLOCKBUSTERS

1937	1994	1995	2010
Snow White and the Seven Dwarfs *kicks off the era of animated feature films.*	The Lion King *is released and eventually becomes the highest-grossing traditionally animated film of all time.*	Toy Story *becomes the first feature-length computer-animated film.*	Toy Story 3 *surpasses Shrek 2 to become the highest-grossing animated film of all time.*

21

PUSHING FORWARD AT PIXAR

Since breaking new ground with *Toy Story*, Pixar has remained a leading computer animation studio. It has released more than a dozen feature-length films. Each one has been a massive box office smash, and almost all of them were well received by critics. In addition to features, Pixar has continued to produce computer-animated short films. Most of these shorts have been nominated for an Academy Award for Best Animated Short Film.

With each new film, Pixar's animators have pushed the boundaries of computer graphics technology. Characters in recent films, such as *Brave* (2012) and *Monsters University* (2013), are more detailed and expressive than ever, and the worlds they inhabit can look almost real.

Pixar animators worked to give each character in Brave *personality, with a range of facial expressions and gestures.*

ENGINEERS HAD TO PROGRAM NEW SOFTWARE TO ANIMATE MERIDA'S CURLY HAIR.

Disney's Frozen *won the Academy Award for best animated film of 2013.*

DISNEY'S NEW DIRECTION

As Pixar led the charge toward a computer-animated future in the 1990s and 2000s, Disney's own animation studios continued to focus on traditionally animated films for many years. While films such as *The Emperor's New Groove* and *Lilo & Stitch* were hits, Disney soon found that many of its hand-drawn films were failing to find wide audiences in a world where computer animation had become the new big thing. It decided to take a new direction with 2005's computer-animated *Chicken Little*. The film was relatively successful, but it did not reach the heights of the computer-animated films being produced by Pixar and other studios.

In 2006, Disney purchased Pixar from Steve Jobs and its other owners. As a result, top Pixar creators such as Ed Catmull and John Lasseter began overseeing all of Disney's animated films, in addition to Pixar's own work. Under their leadership, Walt Disney Animation Studios has released several huge computer-animated hits, including 2012's *Wreck-It Ralph* and 2013's *Frozen*.

MODERN MARVELS

WAYS OF WATCHING

Today, it is possible to watch animated movies, shorts, and TV shows almost anywhere you go, on countless different devices, at any time of day. If you want to see a certain film, all you need to do is find its disc or search for the film on a **streaming** service. However, it hasn't always been so easy to access animated films. At first, the only way to see them was to visit a movie theater. Even short animated films were shown on the big screen, as people did not have equipment to watch films at home. Short cartoons were often shown before feature-length live-action movies as part of a full afternoon or evening of entertainment.

BRINGING IT HOME

Color television became extremely popular during the 1950s and 1960s. Many TV networks began showing animated cartoon shows, including early Hanna-Barbera hits such as *The Huckleberry Hound Show* and *The Yogi Bear Show*. Animated shows have been a major part of television programming ever since, and today there are entire channels that show almost nothing but cartoons.

After Video Home System (VHS) cassettes were introduced in the late 1970s, people were able to rent or purchase tape recordings of their favorite movies. This

Recorded media such as DVDs make it possible to watch movies at home whenever you want to.

Streaming services offer a huge range of movies and television shows to watch.

allowed them to watch animated movies whenever they wanted to. The invention of digital video discs (DVDs) in the 1990s and Blu-ray Discs in the 2000s provided clearer visuals and sound for home recordings. When coupled with a large, high-definition TV screen and a quality sound system, these technologies allowed animation fans to re-create the experience of going to a movie theater right in their own living rooms.

INSTANT ANIMATION

Advances in Internet technology have allowed users to stream high-definition videos over the Web at the push of a button. Viewers can choose almost any animated TV show or movie without ever leaving the couch. They can also stream videos on a range of portable devices, from phones and tablets to laptop computers and video game systems. Thanks to this incredible technology, it is easier than ever to find new animation to watch. It is also easier for up-and-coming animators to find an audience for their work.

DreamWorks co-founder Jeffrey Katzenberg (standing) and musician Bryan Adams (wearing white shirt) discuss the 2002 film Spirit: Stallion of the Cimarron *with a group of animators.*

DREAMS COME TRUE

Many of today's top animated hits come from the wizards at DreamWorks Animation. DreamWorks is a film production company that was established in 1994 by legendary filmmaker Steven Spielberg along with **producers** Jeffrey Katzenberg and David Geffen. The studio released its first two animated films in 1998. *Antz* was computer generated, while *The Prince of Egypt* was created using traditional hand-drawn animation. Both were huge hits, but the studio had an even bigger blockbuster with 2001's *Shrek*. In 2004, DreamWorks spun its animation division off into a separate company. Since then, it has been second only to Pixar in its ability to consistently deliver computer-animated hits at the box office. Among DreamWorks' many success stories are the *Shrek*, *Madagascar*, and *Kung Fu Panda* series.

MORE AND MORE MOVIES

Today, pretty much every major movie studio produces computer-animated movies on a regular basis. One of the most successful has been Blue Sky Studios, which is owned by the film production giant 20th Century Fox and was founded in the 1980s. At first, it focused on creating television commercials and computer-generated effects for live-action films. It began making animated shorts in the late 1990s, and its first feature, *Ice Age*, was released in 2002. The film became a huge hit, spawning several sequels. Since then, Blue Sky has created such hits as *Horton Hears a Who!* (2008), *Rio* (2011), and *Epic* (2013).

Outside of Blue Sky, big computer-animated hits of the past several years include *Cloudy with a Chance of Meatballs* (2009) and its 2013 sequel, both from Sony Pictures Animation, and the *Despicable Me* movies by Universal Pictures and Illumination Entertainment.

In Blue Sky's Epic, *a teenager is transported to a magical, miniature world where good battles evil.*

FROM THIS TO THAT

ELECTRIFYING EFFECTS

Computer animation has grown to be an incredibly powerful tool, not just for people who want to create animated films and TV shows, but also for live-action filmmakers. In the past, filmmakers were limited by the special effects technology that was available to them. Today, computer graphics allow them to put almost anything they can imagine up on the screen. They are limited only by their creativity and ambition.

Harry Potter and the Order of the Phoenix *director David Yates (right) talks with actor Robbie Coltrane (left) in front of a blue screen.*

NEW WORLDS

Live-action movies and TV shows are filmed in real locations and on sets built in movie studios. This makes it easy to film stories that are set in houses, offices, or outdoor areas. However, many films are set in places such as alien worlds, futuristic cities, or the depths of the ocean. It can be difficult and expensive to create these settings in a movie studio. In addition, the results might not look realistic or match the filmmakers' vision. With today's computer graphics technology, however, filmmakers can create impossible worlds. Animators create the settings. Footage of live actors is filmed separately and then layered in with the computer graphics. This technique was put to extensive use in such films as *Avatar* (2009), the *Harry Potter* series, and the *Star Wars* prequels.

BLUE SCREEN, EASILY REPLACED WITH DIGITAL IMAGES

Spider-Man flies through New York City with the help of computer graphics in Spider-Man.

CHARACTERS AND CROWDS

Computer animation can also be used to add unbelievable characters to live-action movies. Characters such as the Hulk in *The Avengers* movies and Gollum in the *The Lord of the Rings* and *The Hobbit* series were created using computer animation. Computer animation can make it look like live-action characters are performing stunts that actors could never do in real life. For example, they can make it seem like Spider-Man is zipping between the buildings of New York City or Superman is flying high in the sky.

Computer animation can also be used to create huge crowds of digital extras. In the past, large crowd scenes required filmmakers to hire dozens or even hundreds of actors. This process can be expensive and time-consuming. Today, filmmakers can simply animate massive groups of extras to fill epic battle scenes or the overflowing streets of a futuristic city.

QUICK FIXES

Computer animation can even be used to solve smaller problems for filmmakers. For example, filmmakers might use computer animation to place an actor's face onto the body of a stunt person. In the past, they might instead have to edit their films to avoid showing a character's face too clearly during a dangerous stunt. Computer animation enables filmmakers to make other small changes after a scene has been shot so they do not have to reshoot footage. While these uses of computer animation are less flashy than big effects, they have become very important to the filmmaking process for many creators. ✳

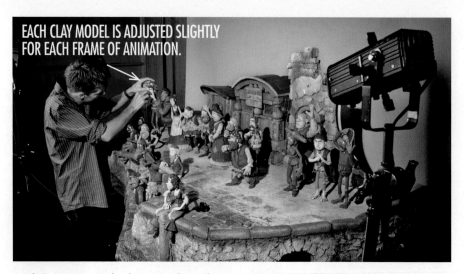

EACH CLAY MODEL IS ADJUSTED SLIGHTLY FOR EACH FRAME OF ANIMATION.

Aardman animator Richard Haynes adjusts characters in preparation for a shot in The Pirates! Band of Misfits.

TRADITIONAL TOONS

Computer-generated animation is more popular than ever, but some animators are sticking to traditional methods of bringing their stories to the big screen. After several years of focusing on computer animation, Disney returned to the world of hand-drawn animation with *The Princess and the Frog* in 2009. Critics praised the film, and audiences were interested in seeing a return to Disney's classic animation style. The movie's positive reception encouraged Disney to continue making hand-drawn films, and it followed *The Princess and the Frog* with 2011's *Winnie the Pooh*.

Some animators continue to use stop-motion techniques. Many of the best-known stop-motion films of recent years have come from Aardman Animations. Aardman became famous during the 1980s and 1990s for the *Wallace & Gromit* short films created by animator Nick Park. The studio released its first stop-motion animated feature, *Chicken Run*, in 2000. Its more recent stop-motion films include *The Pirates! Band of Misfits* (2012) and *Shaun the Sheep* (2015), a feature-length version of the studio's popular television show.

AMAZING ANIME

While traditionally animated feature films have become fairly rare in Hollywood, they have remained more popular in other parts of the world. Hand-drawn animation is especially common in Japan, where it is known as anime. Many of the country's biggest animated movies come from the legendary Studio Ghibli. Founded in 1985, Studio Ghibli is best known for producing the films of animator Hayao Miyazaki, who has often been compared to Walt Disney for his impact on the world of animation. Early hits such as Miyazaki's *My Neighbor Totoro* (1988) and *Kiki's Delivery Service* (1989) helped build the studio's reputation for whimsical storytelling and beautiful hand-drawn artwork. Later successes such as *Princess Mononoke* (1997) and *Spirited Away* (2001) brought even wider acclaim and a massive global audience. Though Miyazaki announced his retirement after the release of 2013's *The Wind Rises*, Studio Ghibli continues to release new films by other directors, including Miyazaki's son, Goro.

Studio Ghibli is famous for its detailed, hand-animated films, such as Princess Mononoke.

ON THE TUBE

Hand-drawn animation remains a major force in the world of television. Millions of viewers tune in to channels such as Nickelodeon and Cartoon Network, where *SpongeBob SquarePants*, *Adventure Time*, and other popular animated shows are aired. These shows are aimed mainly at younger audiences, but kids and adults alike enjoy their colorful animation and lighthearted stories.

Many TV networks also air animated shows aimed at older audiences during the evening hours. Long-running shows such as *The Simpsons* and *Family Guy* continue to attract huge numbers of viewers, while more recent series such as *Bob's Burgers* are building new audiences of animation fans.

Characters Finn the Human and Jake the Dog fly through the air in an episode of Adventure Time.

Actor Neil Patrick Harris plays music with a trio of computer-animated characters in The Smurfs.

BEST OF BOTH WORLDS

Like *Mary Poppins* (1964) and *Who Framed Roger Rabbit* (1988) decades earlier, many of today's films rely on a blend of animation and live-action footage. Disney's 2007 smash *Enchanted* tells the story of animated fairy tale characters who are transported to a live-action world. Some of the movie's scenes were created using hand-drawn animation, while others featured real actors and settings.

The *Alvin and the Chipmunks* and *Smurfs* series both rely on a blend of computer-animated and live-action characters to tell their stories. In these films, computer animation is used to create singing, dancing chipmunks and the tiny blue creatures known as Smurfs. This animation is combined with live-action footage to make it look as though the cartoon characters are living in the real world.

An animator makes a careful adjustment to figures in the stop-motion film Wallace & Gromit: The Curse of the Were-Rabbit.

CHAPTER THREE

CREATIVE MINDS

I n the early days of animation, it was easy for small teams or even hardworking individuals to create films on their own. However, as animated films grew longer and more detailed over time, the number of people required to make them grew substantially. Today's top animated movies are a complex blend of art and technology. Teams made up of dozens or even hundreds of people create them. Each person brings an important set of skills to the team. Some people are the artists and writers who come up with stories and characters. Other team members are the computer programmers and **engineers** who build the latest graphics technology to bring those stories to life in new and exciting ways. There are also actors, directors, composers, sound technicians, and countless other people who all lend their expertise to a project. Together, these people can bring animation magic to screens around the world to enchant and impress audiences.

STUPENDOUS STUDIOS

1930	1972	1985	1986
Warner Bros. Animation is founded.	Aardman Animations opens its doors.	Studio Ghibli opens.	Steve Jobs purchases the Lucasfilm computer graphics division and turns it into Pixar.

Animators and other digital artists can choose a variety of graphics tablets, depending on the task and the artist's preferences.

ALL KINDS OF ARTISTS

Animation is an art form that relies mainly on visuals to tell stories and express ideas. As a result, visual artists are involved in almost every step of the animation process, from the planning stages to the finished product. Some artists rely on digital tools to create their work, while others paint or draw by hand. Even when making a computer-animated film with the latest technology, traditional hand-drawn or painted artwork is involved in some part of the process. For example, concept artists sketch out ideas for what a character, background, or prop might look like in a completed film, while **storyboard** artists often hand-draw pictures to plan out a film's shots before they are animated.

Artists spend years and years developing their style and technique. Many begin drawing and painting when they are very young. Later, most take art classes and study the ways that people, animals, and objects move. This helps them create more realistic movements in their animation. Many artists earn degrees at colleges and universities before becoming professional animators.

ENGINEERING ENTERTAINMENT

Modern animators often use advanced technology, whether they are building 3D worlds or using **software** to animate handmade drawings. Even though animation technology has come a long way, there is always room for improvement. Software developers are the engineers who create the computer programs that animators use to bring ideas to life. They listen to animators' needs and look for new ways to improve programs. For example, an animation team might find that their software is not able to create realistic-looking feathers when they are making a movie about birds. Engineers could write computer code to improve the software or even create new software from scratch. In another situation, they might design new programs to help animators create realistic shadows or reflections. Software developers have strong backgrounds in math and science. They also have in-depth knowledge of the computer programming languages that are used to build software.

New technology is constantly being created to push the envelope of what is possible in animation.

AN INTERVIEW WITH VISUAL DEVELOPMENT ARTIST MICHAEL YAMADA

Michael Yamada is a visual development artist who has worked for DreamWorks Animation, Warner Bros., and other production companies on such films as Puss in Boots, Kung Fu Panda 2, *and* How to Train Your Dragon.

When did you start thinking you wanted to be a concept artist? Did any person or event inspire that career choice? It began for me in middle school at the public library. I happened across several books [while] collecting the art used to make some of my favorite movies. [At] that moment, everything clicked into place, and I realized what I wanted to do.

What kinds of classes should a would-be artist or animator look to take in middle school, high school, and beyond? Take every type of art class that you have time for. A big mistake is only taking classes that sound like exactly what you want [to do]. Take the time to explore, and the experience will pay back in the future.

What other projects and jobs did you do in school and your work life before the opportunity to work in animation came along? How did that work prepare you for your career? I studied product design in school and built physical models of things I designed—ceiling fans, game controllers, the works. It really taught me how things I drew translated into three-dimensional objects.

Do you have a particular project that you're especially proud of, or that you think really took your work to another level? I'm really proud of my work on *Kung Fu Panda 2*. It was my first time working on different parts of the film, and I was thankful for the chance that I was given to do so.

Michael Yamada worked as a visual development artist on Kung Fu Panda 2.

It takes teamwork to create an animated film. Does working as part of a team come naturally to you, or was it something you had to work on? I love being part of a team and learning about what everyone contributes to the movie. I've been a part of several teams, clubs, and groups growing up, and it helped me realize that everyone matters when we're working together.

If you had unlimited resources to work on any project you wanted to, what would you do? I'd love to do my own animated project—probably something episodic like a TV show. I've been slowly working toward achieving that goal and am hoping to achieve part of it soon.

What advice would you give a young person who wants to be a professional artist one day? Always carry a sketchbook with you and be drawing—it doesn't matter if [it is] something around you or something you've made up. It's important to be passionate about your work and to practice it. ✳

3D MODEL MAKERS

The process of creating computer animation is very different from drawing a film by hand. Computer-animated films are not drawn frame by frame. Instead, specially trained artists called 3D modelers create backgrounds, characters, and props using computer software. A 3D model is built of flat shapes called **polygons**. The polygons are arranged to form larger 3D shapes. For example, a cube is made up of six square polygons. The models in a computer-animated movie are usually much more complicated than this, however. A single character model might contain millions of separate shapes! The software used by 3D modelers is often very complex, and it takes a lot of practice to become good at using it.

It takes millions of polygons to create a realistic-looking 3D model.

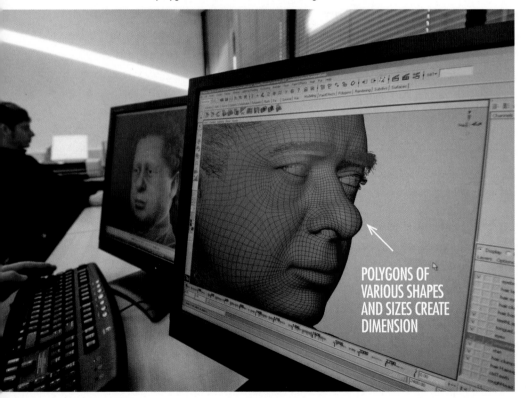

POLYGONS OF VARIOUS SHAPES AND SIZES CREATE DIMENSION

ADDITIONAL SENSORS ON
THE FACE TO CAPTURE THE
ACTOR'S FACIAL EXPRESSIONS

SENSORS AND OPTICAL
MARKERS ATTACHED TO SUITS

Actors Jamie Bell (left) and Andy Serkis (right) perform in motion-capture suits for the animated film The Adventures of Tintin: The Secret of the Unicorn.

AMAZING ANIMATORS

Computer animation teams employ expert animators to create movements for the characters and props that the 3D modelers create. These animators rely on several different methods for putting models into action. For some movements, such as the rolling of car tires or the bouncing of a ball, they might use software to program the motion from scratch. The software uses math and physics to help calculate the way the animated models would move if they were real-life objects.

3D animators also use a process known as motion capture. Actors wear special suits with sensors on them. The sensors match up with specific body parts, and animators can record the sensors' movements. They can then attach these recorded movements to the corresponding body parts of 3D character models. This allows them to animate people and animals to appear lifelike.

THE ARTISTIC SIDE

Musician and actress Taylor Swift records her voice for a character in Dr. Seuss' The Lorax.

SIGHTS AND SOUNDS

Ever since animators first started using synchronized soundtracks in the 1920s, voice, sound effects, and music have played an important role in animated films of all kinds. With powerful surround sound systems installed in theaters and living rooms around the world, quality sound is more important than ever. Filmmakers rely on the efforts of many talented artists to provide the noises and voices that make up a movie soundtrack.

SILVER TONGUES

Most popular animated movies today rely heavily on spoken **dialogue** to tell stories and develop characters. Filmmakers rely on the work of talented voice-over actors to put words in their characters' mouths. Performing **voice-overs** is very different from acting on-screen. Voice-over actors must express themselves entirely through their voices. However, the actors' movements are not ignored. Actors are often videotaped during recording sessions so animators can later watch the video and imitate a gesture or facial expression.

Many professional voice-over actors can alter their voices to play an incredible variety of different roles. Because they do not appear on-screen, they might even play several roles in the same movie or show.

MERRY MELODIES

Music is also an important part of an animated film's soundtrack. It can be used to help set the mood of a scene or add excitement to the on-screen action. Sometimes filmmakers choose popular songs from their own music collections to soundtrack their movies. Other times, they work with composers to create a **score**. Some animated films are musicals. This means that the characters sing songs to help move the story forward. In these cases, songwriters work closely with the filmmakers to write the lyrics that the characters will sing.

Composer Thomas Newman conducts an orchestra playing the score to Pixar's WALL-E.

Foley artists produce the sounds of a swimming sea monster.

CREAKS, CRACKS, AND RATTLES

Because there are no real objects to make noises in an animated movie, all of the sound effects must be added separately, from the clomping of boots on pavement to the rattling bones of a dancing skeleton. Sometimes these noises can simply be selected from recorded libraries of common sound effects or designed using computer software. Other times, professionals called Foley artists create the sounds from scratch. Foley artists use any objects they can find to create just the right sound effects for what is happening on-screen. They might throw heavy objects into containers full of water to create the sound of a character jumping into a pool. Or they might slap pieces of meat together to make the sound of a superhero punching an enemy. The possibilities are endless! ✸

A lighting artist brightens and darkens areas of an animated scene, adjusting the lighting depending on the scene's location and time of day.

SHADOWS AND SURFACES

Freshly created 3D models don't look like the final images you see when you watch a movie. They have flat surfaces without any color or texture. Texture artists design the outer appearance of 3D models, from the smooth skin of a young character's face to the rough bark of a gnarled old tree.

Lighting artists also add important details to computer-generated scenes. They design the way light sources in a scene create shadows and reflections on the surfaces of characters, backgrounds, and props. This process can make or break the way an animated film turns out. Bad lighting will look strange to viewers and make it difficult for them to follow the action on the screen. However, quality lighting can greatly improve the look of even very basic 3D models.

PLANNING A PRODUCTION

Not all of the people who work on an animated film are visual artists or computer experts. Just like live-action movies and TV shows, animated films rely on the guidance of writers and directors. Writers are responsible for creating an animated film's script. A script is a typed document containing all of a film's dialogue, as well as basic descriptions of settings and character actions.

A director works from the script to oversee the creation of the movie. He or she usually has the final say in all creative decisions. For example, the director might decide how characters deliver their lines, where the "camera" is in each shot, or whether certain scenes need to be cut or added. He or she also determines where characters are positioned in a shot and what movements they make. Directors must be able to visualize shots in their minds and communicate these ideas to the team's artists and actors.

Director Dan Scanlon (front) discusses the movie Monsters University *with graphic artist Cassandra Smolcic and production designer Ricky Nierva.*

Filmmaker John Lasseter arrives at the world premiere of Monsters University in 2013.

4

BRINGING IDEAS TO LIFE

E ven with a talented team of hardworking professionals, creating an animated film can be a long, difficult process. Each film is a major investment for the studio. Animated features from major movie studios can cost tens or even hundreds of millions of dollars to create. This places a great deal of pressure on the filmmakers to deliver a movie that will draw in audiences and make back the money that was spent to make it. Filmmakers often face tight time constraints as well, as studios rush to release their biggest hits during peak movie-going seasons. With so much on the line, it is no wonder that filmmakers follow a careful process to create big-budget animated movies.

DARING DEBUTS

1930	1984	1986	2000
Warner Bros. releases "Sinkin' in the Bathtub," the first Looney Tunes *cartoon.*	Pixar releases its first computer-animated short film, The Adventures of André and Wally B.	Hayao Miyazaki's Castle in the Sky *is the first film to be released by Studio Ghibli.*	Aardman releases its first feature-length film, Chicken Run.

Producing a script can require a lot of writing, rewriting, and collaboration.

WRITING IT DOWN

The first step in creating a new film is developing an idea for a story. This is often a collaborative process between writers, directors, and producers. Studios and investors consider whether a story is likely to attract an audience before they agree to make a movie. This is why many animated films are based on popular books, comics, or other sources. These stories already have fans who will want to see the animated versions of their favorite characters. However, some of the most successful animated films were made using original characters and stories.

Once the filmmakers have settled on a story idea, it is time for writers to create a script. Sometimes a single person writes the script. Other times, an entire team works together to write a movie. Scripts often go through many revisions before they are completed. Producers and the director might suggest ideas along the way.

PLOTTING OUT SHOTS

Once a final script has been approved, the director and producers begin working with storyboard artists to plan what each shot of the movie will look like. A storyboard for a feature-length film might be made up of hundreds of individual images. The images might be done by hand or created using computer software. Either way, the images are posted up on boards and hung on the wall so the filmmakers can see how each shot flows into the next. The director can make changes to each shot. For example, he or she might decide to zoom in more for a certain shot or change the order of two scenes in order to make the story flow better.

Once the storyboard is close to being final, the editor turns them into a simple animation called a story reel. The editor might add placeholder sounds to the story reel to get a better idea of what it will be like to watch the final product. The filmmakers continue making tweaks to the story reel until they have a very strong idea of how every shot of the movie will look.

Director Chris Wedge checks details in Ice Age *storyboards.*

WHERE THE MAGIC HAPPENS

Animator Andreas Deja discusses animation at a Disney conference.

WALT DISNEY ANIMATION STUDIOS

For more than 75 years, Walt Disney Animation Studios has been at the forefront of animation. Its talented artists, technicians, and storytellers have created dozens of groundbreaking films, from 1937's *Snow White and the Seven Dwarfs* to 2013's *Frozen*.

TOP TALENT

As one of today's top animation studios, Disney recruits some of the world's most talented animators. However, even the greatest animators in the world can find ways to improve their skills. Disney Animation employees develop their abilities by taking classes taught by the studio's expert animators. They might learn how to use the latest graphics software, expand their artistic abilities, or study filmmaking techniques.

TOMORROW'S ANIMATION SUPERSTARS

Disney is constantly on the lookout for tomorrow's animation pioneers. It offers a variety of internships to students who dream of breaking into the world of animation. These programs give the students a chance to work beside some of the greatest animators in the world and get an up close look at how animated films are made. An internship lasts for a set period of time and offers training in a specialized topic. For example, one internship might have the student learning to create realistic fur for animated animals, while another might offer instruction on animating smoke. These positions are highly competitive, with some of the world's best and brightest students competing for a spot on the team.

SHARING KNOWLEDGE

Disney is constantly working to improve its technology. As its employees develop new technological breakthroughs, they document their findings by writing papers and creating demonstrations. They present their findings at conferences and publish them in journals so other animators can use them and possibly even make improvements of their own. This helps push animation technology forward at a fast rate.

The Association for Computing Machinery hosts conferences on computer graphics technology around the world each year.

GOOD LOOKS

As the filmmakers are deciding how their movie will flow from one shot to the next, other artists are hard at work designing the characters, props, and backgrounds that will appear in the film. This phase is known as a film's visual development. During visual development, the artists create drawings, paintings, or even sculptures of everything that will appear in the film. As they work, the director and producers make suggestions for improvements. For example, they might ask to see what it would look like if a character was taller or had a different hairstyle. Different clothing might change the way viewers think of a certain character, and different colors might change the feel of a setting. Every visual detail is taken into careful consideration.

A sketch from the production of How to Train Your Dragon *shows simple early visions of main character Hiccup (right) and his dragon, Toothless.*

An animator checks proxies during production of Shrek the Third.

SMOOTH MOVES

Modelers use the approved designs created by the visual development artists to begin creating the 3D models that will actually appear on-screen. Each component that a modeler creates is called an asset. Modelers start by creating simple, less-detailed versions of the assets called proxies, without textures or lighting. CG, or computer graphic, layout artists put all the necessary proxies together for a shot and establish camera moves. The director watches this rough footage and requests any tweaks that need to be made. Once a scene is approved, the proxies are replaced with more detailed versions. Then artists add textures, lighting, and other visual effects.

When making traditionally animated films, some artists might specialize in painting beautiful backgrounds, while others draw characters and props. Originally, characters and props were inked and colored by hand on **cels**, which were placed over the finished painted background before being filmed. Today, software programs have replaced the process of inking and painting by hand.

LASTING CONTRIBUTIONS

3D glasses made of blue and red lenses were used throughout the last half of the 20th century.

POPPING OUT OF THE SCREEN

In recent years, 3D effects have been among the most popular additions to animated films. Thanks to the latest projection technology, animated characters and objects can look as though they are popping right out of movie and TV screens. But while today's 3D movies make use of sophisticated technology, 3D films have actually existed since the 1920s. They have come a long way since then, but the basic principles behind them have stayed the same.

HOW IT WORKS

3D movies use a process called **stereoscopy**. This means that each of your eyes sees a different image when it focuses on the screen. This makes it seem as if there is depth to the image. The effect is created by projecting two images onto a screen at the same time. Originally, one image was tinted red, and the other was tinted blue. 3D glasses had one blue-tinted lens and one red-tinted lens. This allowed each eye to see just one of the projections at a time. Modern 3D films use a much more complicated system that provides a clearer picture, better colors, and easier viewing.

3D EVERYWHERE

Today, almost every major animated film—along with many live-action films—is released in a 3D version. Special 3DTVs and 3D Blu-ray Discs even allow fans to watch their favorite movies in 3D at home. Some studios have begun making 3D versions of older hits. For example, Disney has released 3D editions of the stop-motion classic *The Nightmare Before Christmas* (1993, re-released in 2006) and hand-drawn hits such as *The Lion King* (1994, re-released in 2011) and *Beauty and the Beast* (1991, re-released in 2013). These re-releases draw audiences into theaters to get a fresh look at old favorites. ✳

3D technology has been used in a huge variety of animated films.

TUNES AND TALKING

As the movie's visuals start to come together and resemble something that could be shown in a theater, the team can begin developing the final soundtrack. A composer might watch portions of the movie and speak with the filmmakers to get a feel for what kinds of music will work best in each scene. The director and producers work to cast voice-over actors who fit their roles perfectly.

Sound engineers combine the score, voice-overs, and various sound effects to create the movie's final soundtrack. They adjust the volume of each part of the soundtrack to make sure dialogue is not drowned out by music or background sounds. They might also adjust sounds to make them seem as if they are coming from certain directions. This helps immerse the audience in the film's world.

Sound engineers adjust a film's many sounds to find the perfect balance.

Animators hope to entertain their audiences as much as possible.

OPENING NIGHT

As the filmmakers put the finishing touches on their creation, the movie studio begins promoting the film to audiences. Posters, television advertisements, and trailers highlight the most exciting aspects of the movie and help generate interest from the public. With any luck, viewers will pack theaters when the movie hits the big screen on opening night.

After a short vacation, it is time for the team to start working on its next project. If the earlier film was a big success, the studio might ask for a sequel to be made. Or perhaps the writers and director have a brand-new idea for the next big thing. Either way, there are always new stories to be told and new advances to be made in animation.

THE FUTURE

Characters from Inside Out *include, from left to right, Fear, Sadness, Joy, Disgust, and Anger.*

THE FUTURE

Like any form of technology, animation is constantly evolving. Animation techniques and special effects that blow audiences away today might look run-of-the-mill or even outdated in just a few years. Some future animation developments are easy to predict. Engineers and artists will keep looking for new ways to make models more detailed and lighting more natural, making computer graphics more realistic. They will refine motion capture technology to pick up the actors' slightest movements, allowing for more lifelike, expressive performances from animated characters. Other aspects of the technology are more difficult to predict. The animators of the early 20th century could not have known what animation would become a century later, and we can only imagine where it will go from here.

TOMORROW'S BLOCKBUSTERS

The world's top animation studios are constantly hard at work on the next wave of animated feature films. Pixar's *Inside Out* takes place inside the mind of a young girl. Disney's *Big Hero 6* is based on a popular Marvel Comics superhero team, while Warner Bros.' *The Lego Movie* gives viewers a combination of computer animation and stop-motion animation using real Lego toys. The filmmakers claim that their computer animation is so realistic audiences can't tell the difference between the real Lego pieces and the computer-animated ones. All in all, the studios are showing no signs of slowing down.

The Lego Movie *was a big success in theaters.*

Future animators can start playing with and learning animation technology early on.

EASIER THAN EVER

Though major studios dominate the world of animated film and television, it is easier than ever for smaller teams or even individuals to create and share animated works with audiences around the globe. The hardware and software needed to create animation is far more affordable than it was in the past, and Web sites such as YouTube make it easy to post videos online where anyone can watch them. Creative young animators are using this innovative and exciting technology to spread their stories, ideas, and techniques. ✳

CAREER STATS

MULTIMEDIA ARTISTS AND ANIMATORS

MEDIAN ANNUAL SALARY (2010): $58,510

NUMBER OF JOBS (2010): 66,500

PROJECTED JOB GROWTH: 8%, slower than average

PROJECTED INCREASE IN JOBS 2010–2020: 5,500

REQUIRED EDUCATION: Bachelor's degree in art, computer graphics, computer programming, or a related field

LICENSE/CERTIFICATION: Certification may be necessary for certain jobs

PRODUCERS AND DIRECTORS

MEDIAN ANNUAL SALARY (2010): $68,440

NUMBER OF JOBS (2010): 122,500

PROJECTED JOB GROWTH: 11%, average

PROJECTED INCREASE IN JOBS 2010–2020: 13,500

REQUIRED EDUCATION: Bachelor's degree

LICENSE/CERTIFICATION: None

COMPUTER PROGRAMMERS

MEDIAN ANNUAL SALARY (2010): $71,380

NUMBER OF JOBS (2010): 363,100

PROJECTED JOB GROWTH: 12%, average

PROJECTED INCREASE IN JOBS 2010–2020: 43,700

REQUIRED EDUCATION: Bachelor's degree required for most jobs, but some positions require only an associate's degree

LICENSE/CERTIFICATION: Certification may provide an advantage when competing for jobs but is not generally required

Figures reported by the United States Bureau of Labor Statistics

RESOURCES

BOOKS

Bliss, John. *Art That Moves: Animation Around the World.* Chicago: Raintree, 2011.

Lenburg, Jeff. *Walt Disney: The Mouse That Roared.* New York: Chelsea House Publishers, 2011.

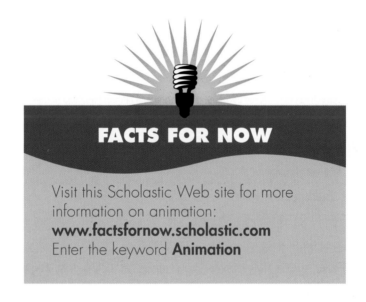

FACTS FOR NOW

Visit this Scholastic Web site for more information on animation:
www.factsfornow.scholastic.com
Enter the keyword **Animation**

GLOSSARY

cels (SELZ) transparent sheets of plastic on which objects are drawn or painted in the making of animated films

computer graphics (kuhm-PYOO-tur GRAF-iks) the pictures or images that can be made on a computer

dialogue (DYE-uh-log) conversation, especially in a play, movie, television program, or book

engineers (en-juh-NEERZ) people who are specially trained to design and build machines, large structures, or computer software and hardware

exposure (ik-SPOH-zhur) a piece of film that reveals a photographic image when it is exposed to light

film (FILM) a roll of thin plastic that you put in a camera to take photographs or motion pictures

frame (FRAME) one of the images on a strip of film that make up a moving picture

hardware (HAHRD-wair) computer equipment

live-action (LIVE AK-shuhn) describing a film in which real people or animals perform

polygons (PAH-li-gahnz) shapes with three or more sides; triangles, squares, pentagons, and hexagons are all polygons

producers (proh-DOOS-urz) people in charge of financing and putting on a play or making a movie or TV program

projectors (pruh-JEK-turz) machines that show slides or movies on a screen

reel (REEL) a spool for photographic film

score (SKOR) a written piece of music

software (SAWFT-wair) computer programs that control the workings of the equipment, or hardware, and direct it to do specific tasks

sprocket (SPRAH-kit) a wheel with a rim made of toothlike points that fit into the holes of a chain or filmstrip

stereoscopy (ster-ee-AH-skuh-pee) the seeing of objects in three dimensions

storyboard (STOR-ee-bord) a panel or series of panels with sketches, arranged to show the sequence of camera shots in a film, television show, or other production

streaming (STREEM-ing) watching or listening to music at the same time that it is being downloaded to a computer

voice-overs (VOIS-oh-vurz) recorded voices

INDEX

Page numbers in *italics* indicate illustrations.

INDEX (CONTINUED)

ABOUT THE AUTHOR

JOSH GREGORY writes and edits books for kids. He lives in Chicago, Illinois.